CLIMATE AND WEATHER:

WHAT'S THE DIFFERENCE?

Instruments and Forecasts | Children's Books on Weather Grade 5
Children's Weather Books

BABY PROFESSOR
EDUCATION KIDS

First Edition, 2019

Published in the United States by Speedy Publishing LLC, 40 E Main Street, Newark, Delaware 19711 USA.

© 2019 Baby Professor Books, an imprint of Speedy Publishing LLC

All rights reserved.

Without limiting the rights under the copyright reserved above, no part of this publication may be reproduced, stored in or introduced into a retrieval system, or transmitted, in any form, or by any means (electronic, mechanical, photocopying, recording, or otherwise), without the prior written permission of the copyright owner.

All images in this book have been reproduced with the knowledge and prior consent of the artists concerned, and no responsibility is accepted by producer, publisher, or printer for any infringement of copyright or otherwise arising from the contents of this publication.

Baby Professor Books are available at special discounts when purchased in bulk for industrial and sales-promotional use. For details contact our Special Sales Team at Speedy Publishing LLC, 40 E Main Street, Newark, Delaware 19711 USA. Telephone (888) 248-4521 Fax: (210) 519-4043. www.speedybookstore.com

10 9 8 7 6 * 5 4 3 2 1

Print Edition: 9781541949423
Digital Edition: 9781541951228

See the world in pictures. Build your knowledge in style.
https://www.speedypublishing.com/

TABLE OF CONTENTS

In this book, we're going to talk about the difference between climate and weather, so let's get right to it!

WHAT IS THE DIFFERENCE BETWEEN CLIMATE AND WEATHER?

MON	TUE	WED	THU	FRI	SAT
25°	29°	30°	23°	22°	20°

Weather changes from minute to minute and from day to day. Some days are sunny and other days it's rainy. Weather describes what's happening in the atmosphere in a particular area over a short period of time from minutes to weeks. The weather is different everywhere on the planet.

Different Weather Icons

On the other hand, climate is the description of the average weather patterns of a region over a longer period of time. The time period could range from seasons to a span of thirty years.

So, when we're discussing climate, we mean the average weather pattern over the long term. One way to think of climate is the way the weather "behaves" in a certain region over a long period of time.

Climate Change

For example, let's say you are visiting a friend in Yuma, Arizona during the winter. On the day you get there, it's raining. But, later in the day it turns sunny and it gets quite warm. At night, the temperatures get rather cold. This is a description of the weather.

The sudden change of weather

However, if you were asked to describe the pattern of weather "behavior" in Yuma, Arizona throughout the year, you would definitely come to the conclusion that Yuma has a sunny climate.

Desert Winter Morning in Yuma Arizona

The reason is that the overall data would show sunny weather there from sunrise to sunset about 90% of the time. Yuma has an arid climate, which simply means it's located in the desert and has little rainfall. It's actually been declared the sunniest city in the United States.

WHAT IS CLIMATE CHANGE?

MON	TUE	WED	THU	FRI	SAT
25°	29°	30°	23°	22°	20°

Have your parents or grandparents ever told you a story about how they had to walk to school in waist-high snow when they were younger? Maybe you've never seen that much snow and as a result you didn't believe their stories.

A man shoveling deep snow

The reality is that the pattern of snowfall has changed across the United States and in other areas of the world since your parents or grandparents were your age. This change has taken place over several decades so it's a climate change.

Snowfall has changed across the United States and in other areas of the world

Thermometer shows the temperature is hot in the sky, Summer

In some areas of the world people have noticed that temperatures in the summer are hotter and that the spring season is coming earlier compared to thirty years ago. These differences signal a change in climate.

Toxic waste from human hands Industries that create pollution and cities that are affected by pollution

Many factors cause climate changes. Usually climate change has happened very gradually over a span of thousands if not millions of years. However, due to human-generated pollution, our climate is in the process of changing much more rapidly than before.

Here are some of the factors that influence climate changes:

• The heat from the sun

The sun's heat varies as does the potential for Earth's atmosphere to either reflect or absorb it.

Heat of the sun

The changes in the Earth's orbit

Sometimes the Earth's orbit is closer to the sun and sometimes it's farther away.

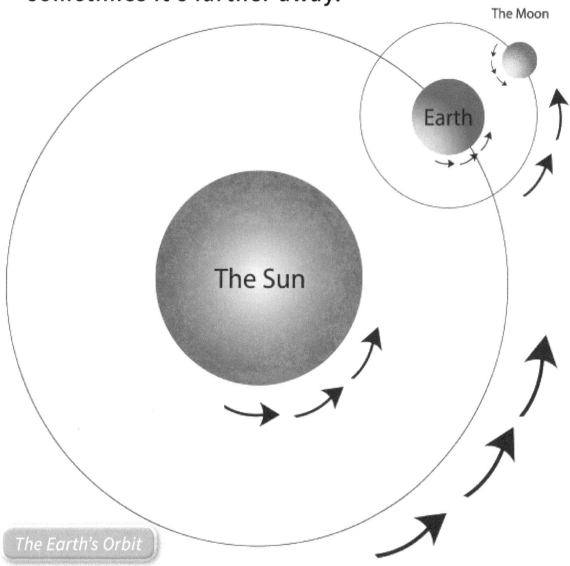

The Moon

Earth

The Sun

The Earth's Orbit

• The angle of the axis of rotation

When the angle of Earth's rotation increases, the winters become colder and the summers hotter.

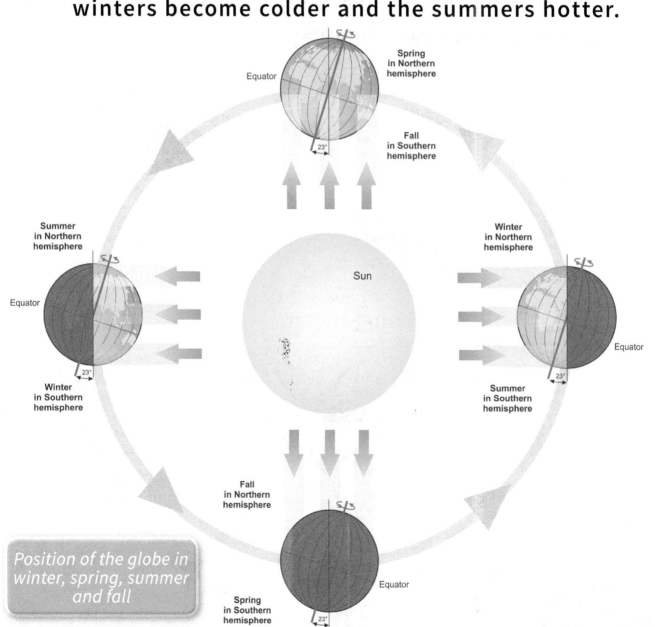

Position of the globe in winter, spring, summer and fall

• The amount of greenhouse gases

Carbon dioxide, water vapor, and methane are being pumped into the atmosphere. The increase in greenhouse gases frequently comes from pollution caused by humans.

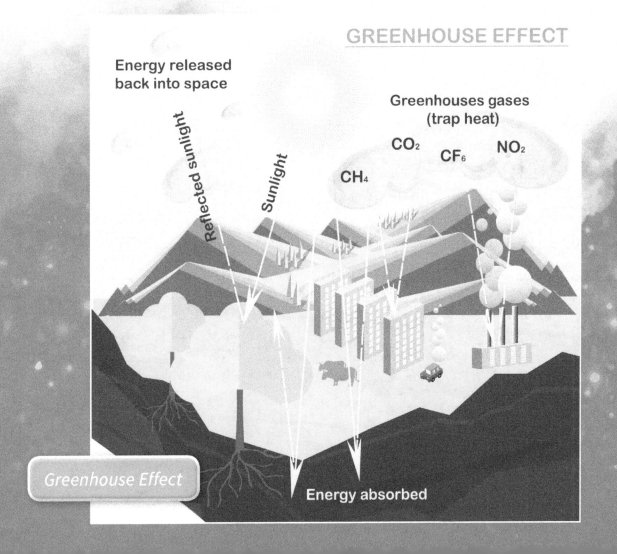

GREENHOUSE EFFECT

Energy released back into space

Greenhouses gases (trap heat)

CO_2

CF_6

NO_2

CH_4

Reflected sunlight

Sunlight

Energy absorbed

Greenhouse Effect

When carbon dioxide is trapped in the ocean it doesn't increase the heat, but if it moves into the atmosphere it traps heat from solar radiation. As a result, the climate's temperature continues to get hotter and hotter.

Global Carbon Cycle

• The movement of the Earth's tectonic plates and eruptions from volcanoes

For example, the position of Great Britain was closer to the equator millions of years ago than it is today. Therefore, at that time its climate was much hotter.

Map plate tectonics world

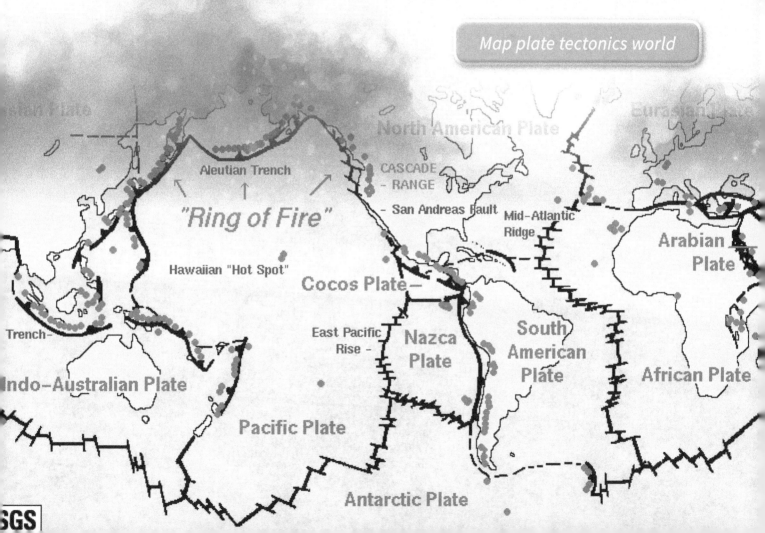

North American Plate

Eurasian Plate

Aleutian Trench

CASCADE - RANGE

San Andreas Fault

Mid-Atlantic Ridge

"Ring of Fire"

Arabian Plate

Hawaiian "Hot Spot"

Cocos Plate —

East Pacific Rise -

Nazca Plate

South American Plate

African Plate

Trench-

Indo-Australian Plate

Pacific Plate

Antarctic Plate

GS

• The movement of ocean currents

When ocean currents shift they bring more heat to different areas of the Earth. The shift in temperature can cause El Niño, which brings on lots of rain, or La Niña, which also changes weather patterns.

Ocean currents

• The amount of vegetation on land

Vegetation tends to absorb carbon dioxide, which helps minimize the chance for increased global warming.

Rainforest

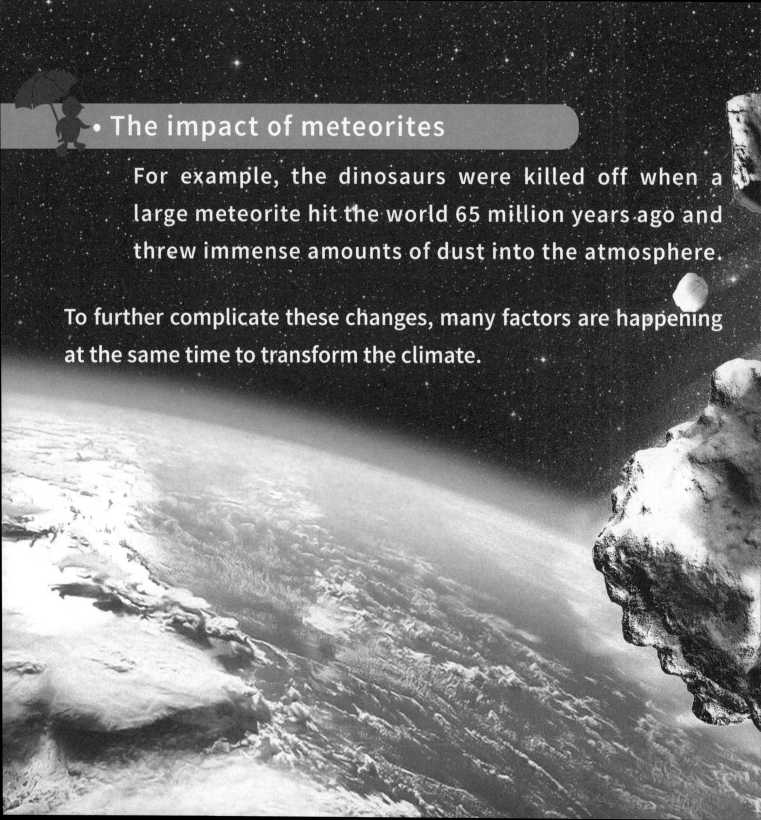

• The impact of meteorites

For example, the dinosaurs were killed off when a large meteorite hit the world 65 million years ago and threw immense amounts of dust into the atmosphere.

To further complicate these changes, many factors are happening at the same time to transform the climate.

Meteor hit the world 65 million years ago

HOW IS CLIMATE MEASURED

MON	TUE	WED	THU	FRI	SAT
25°	29°	30°	23°	22°	20°

Climatologists are climate scientists. They collect data from Earth's soil, air, and water to analyze weather patterns. They also collect information from ice cores and from plant life in different regions.

Scientist reporting on climate change conference ecology concept

CLIMATE CHANGE

They study data that is available from meteorological stations. They use the weather data along with images from radar and satellites to predict climate changes. They often use computer simulations and models to forecast these changes in climate.

Group of scientists investigating hurricane as consequence of global warming on earth.

WHAT ARE THE CHARACTERISTICS OF WEATHER?

MON	TUE	WED	THU	FRI	SAT
25°	29°	30°	23°	22°	20°

Depending on where you live, the weather changes from season to season. Temperature is one measurement that we almost always think of when we think of the weather.

Meteorological weather map of the United State of America

Another variable that impacts the weather is the speed of the wind. When it's cold outdoors, the wind speed can make it feel even colder.

Cold weather, winter mist covered the mountain

When it's hot outdoors, if the humidity is high but it hasn't rained it can feel even hotter.

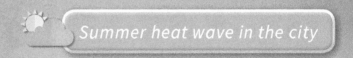 *Summer heat wave in the city*

If you live in a rainy or snowy area, you are probably more aware of all the different types of precipitation, such as rain, ice, sleet, snow, or hail.

Rainy or snowy area

The many types of clouds are also clues to daily weather and play a huge part in forecasting upcoming weather. There are also catastrophic forms of weather, such as hurricanes, tornadoes, and floods.

Dark storm clouds before rain

Hurricane

Tornado

Flood

HOW DO METEOROLOGISTS FORECAST THE WEATHER?

MON	TUE	WED	THU	FRI	SAT

25°	29°	30°	23°	22°	20°

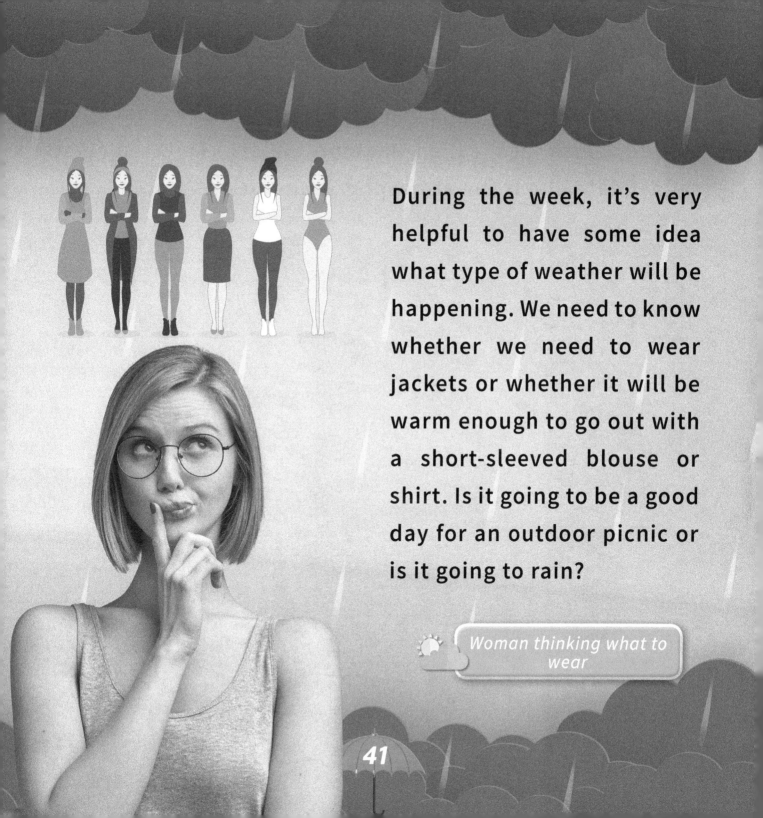

During the week, it's very helpful to have some idea what type of weather will be happening. We need to know whether we need to wear jackets or whether it will be warm enough to go out with a short-sleeved blouse or shirt. Is it going to be a good day for an outdoor picnic or is it going to rain?

Woman thinking what to wear

Scientists who study the atmosphere in different locations around Earth are called meteorologists. Meteorologists collect data about the atmospheric conditions

Meteorologist reading meteodata instruments in modern meteorologic observation station

By studying this data, they can predict what the weather might be over a period of days. Of course, the weather is changeable and there are dozens of different variables so these forecasts are rarely 100% correct.

WHY IS AIR PRESSURE IMPORTANT?

MON	TUE	WED	THU	FRI	SAT

25°	29°	30°	23°	22°	20°

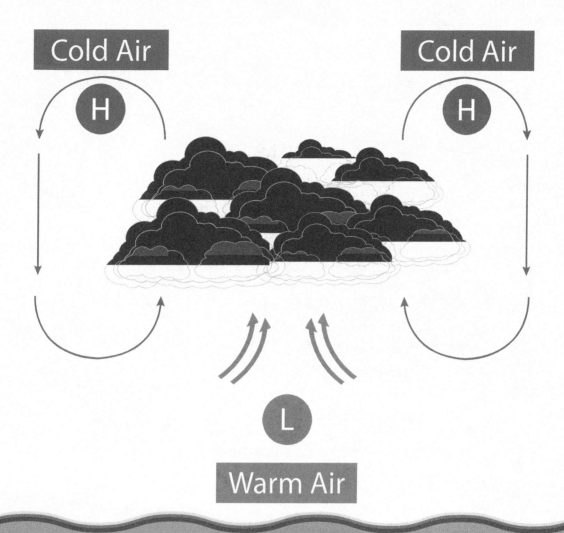

Cold Air

H

Cold Air

H

L

Warm Air

Variances in air pressure are critical to forecasting the weather. The reason is that air pressure is what makes wind form. Systems of high pressure tend to mean that good weather will be forecasted.

 Air Pressure

These systems attract cooler air that's also dry. When a meteorologist makes a forecast he or she will use a blue "H" to represent a high-pressure system on a map. A system of low pressure typically indicates that rainy or stormy weather is on the way. These systems bring in warm air that's also filled with moist water vapor. Meteorologists use a red "L" to represent this type of system on the map.

Meteorological forecast

WHAT IS A WEATHER FRONT?

MON	TUE	WED	THU	FRI	SAT

25°	29°	30°	23°	22°	20°

If you've ever watched the weather report on television, you've probably noticed that the map is a pattern of high-pressure and low-pressure systems. The places where these systems meet are called fronts.

Weather Forecaster

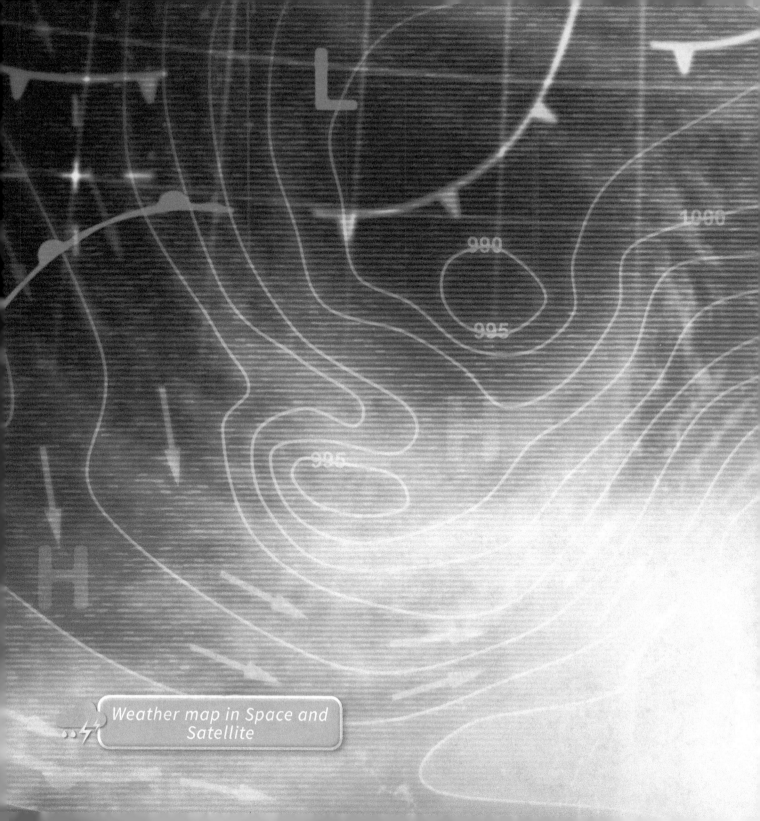

Weather map in Space and Satellite

Most storms happen at the boundaries between high-pressure and low-pressure systems. Depending on the movement and types of these fronts they are described in different ways.

Cold fronts bring cold air with them and they push underneath a mass of warm air, which causes it to rise. The temperature decreases when they blow through. These types of fronts cause rapid changes in the weather and they frequently cause a narrow edge of storms, but as they move through, they generally bring cool, pleasant weather.

Direction of Front

COLD FRONT

COLD AIR

WARM AIR

Cold Front

Warm fronts bring warm air, which slides up and over cold air. They have a tendency to move through at a slower pace than fronts of cold air. They often bring humidity, rain, cloudy weather, or light snow, which is followed by milder, warmer weather.

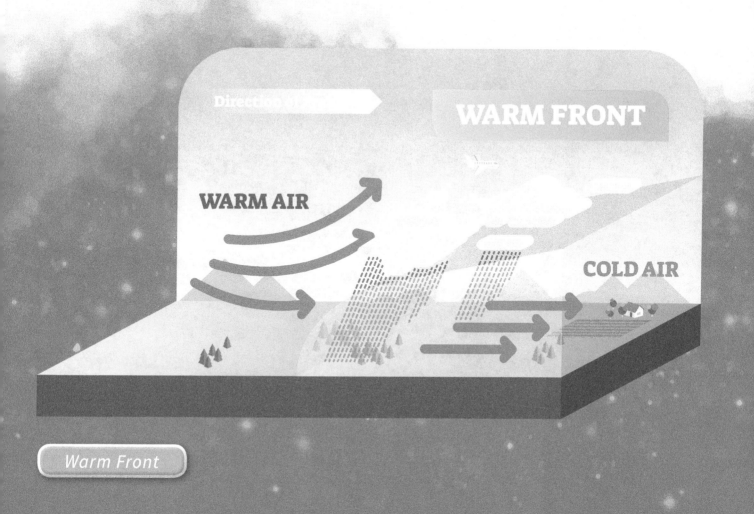

Warm Front

Stationary fronts are parked in one place for a long time period. As the warm air and cold air meet they are balanced so they don't move each other. Clouds and fog form and it sometimes rains or snows. These fronts can bring long seasons of rainy weather.

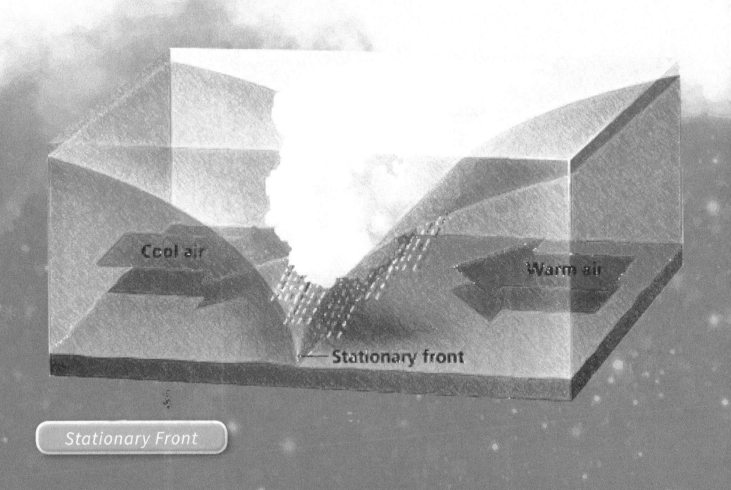

Cool air

Warm air

Stationary front

Stationary Front

Occluded fronts occur when a mass of warm air is trapped between two masses of cold air. As the warm air is separated from the ground, the temperature drops. These types of fronts can bring on strong winds and heavy rains or snow.

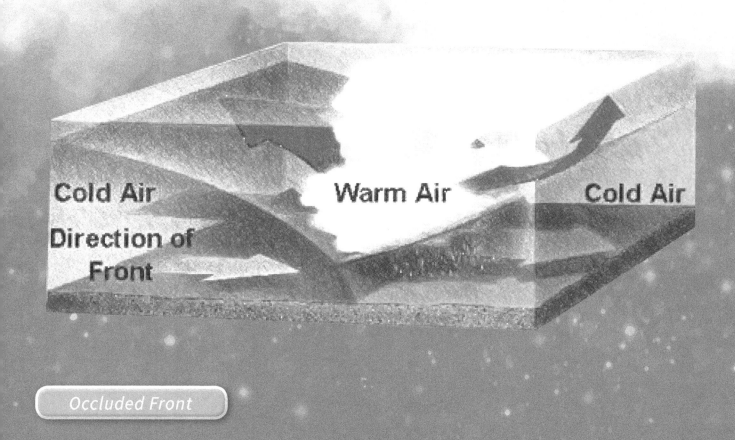

Cold Air

Warm Air

Cold Air

Direction of Front

Occluded Front

WHAT INSTRUMENTS ARE USED TO MEASURE THE WEATHER?

MON	TUE	WED	THU	FRI	SAT

25°	29°	30°	23°	22°	20°

Meteorologists use lots of different high-tech instruments to measure the weather and then forecast future weather.

• A thermometer is used to measure the outdoor temperature from below freezing to sun-scorched. The coldest temperature ever recorded on Earth was **minus** 128.6 degrees Fahrenheit and the hottest temperature was 134.1 degrees Fahrenheit.

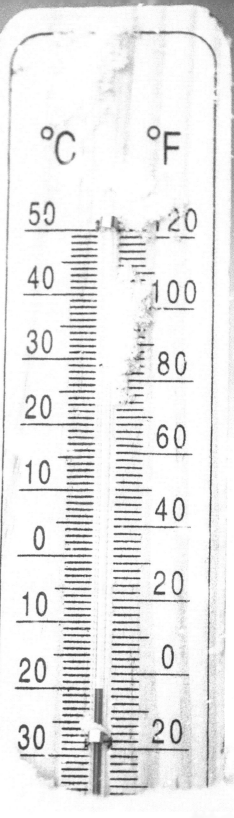

Thermometer

• A rain gauge is used to calculate the amount of rain that's fallen.

Rain Gauge

- An anemometer is used to measure wind speed.

Anemometer

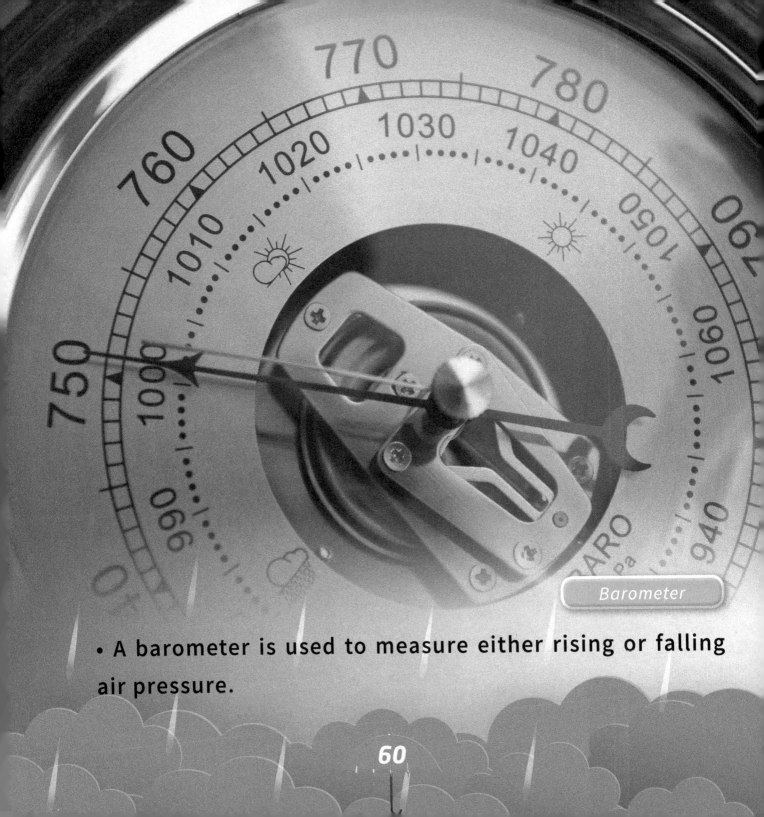

Barometer

• A barometer is used to measure either rising or falling air pressure.

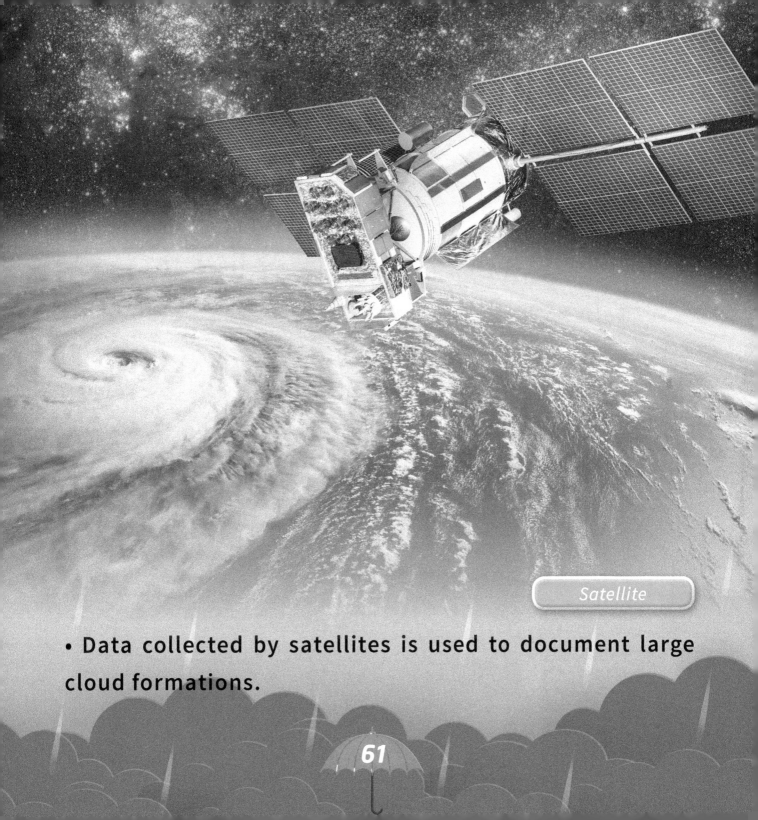

Satellite

• Data collected by satellites is used to document large cloud formations.

• Doppler radar is used to calculate both the speed and the direction of different forms of precipitation such as rain, snow, or hail. It's also used to calculate the speed as well as the direction of the wind. Meteorologists use Doppler radar to provide advance warning for severe thunderstorms or tornadoes.

Doppler Radar

Boston, MA Weather Radar

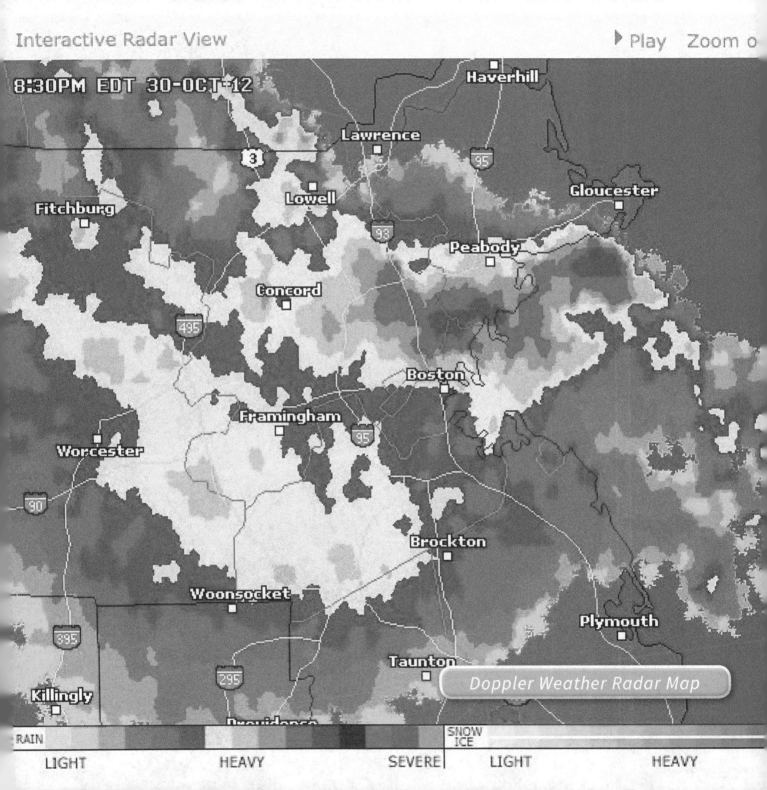

Interactive Radar View ▸ Play Zoom o

8:30PM EDT 30-OCT-12

Haverhill

Lawrence

95

Fitchburg

Lowell

Gloucester

93

Peabody

Concord

495

Boston

Framingham

95

Worcester

90

Brockton

Woonsocket

Plymouth

395

Taunton

295

Doppler Weather Radar Map

Killingly

Providence

RAIN

LIGHT HEAVY SEVERE

SNOW ICE

LIGHT HEAVY

SUMMARY

MON	TUE	WED	THU	FRI	SAT
25°	29°	30°	23°	22°	20°

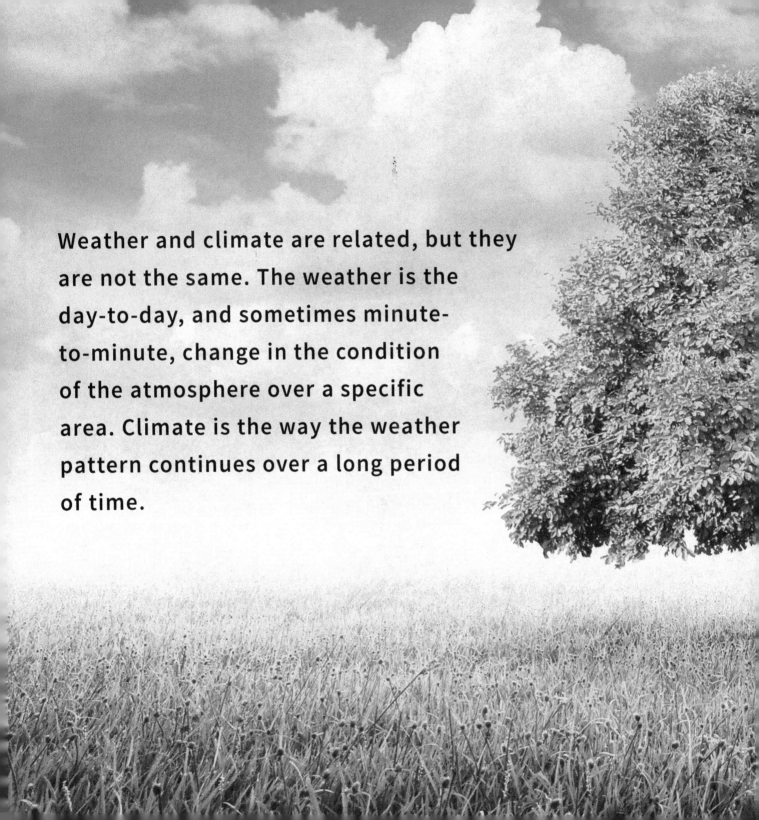

Weather and climate are related, but they are not the same. The weather is the day-to-day, and sometimes minute-to-minute, change in the condition of the atmosphere over a specific area. Climate is the way the weather pattern continues over a long period of time.

Plants and climate change with the concept of global warming

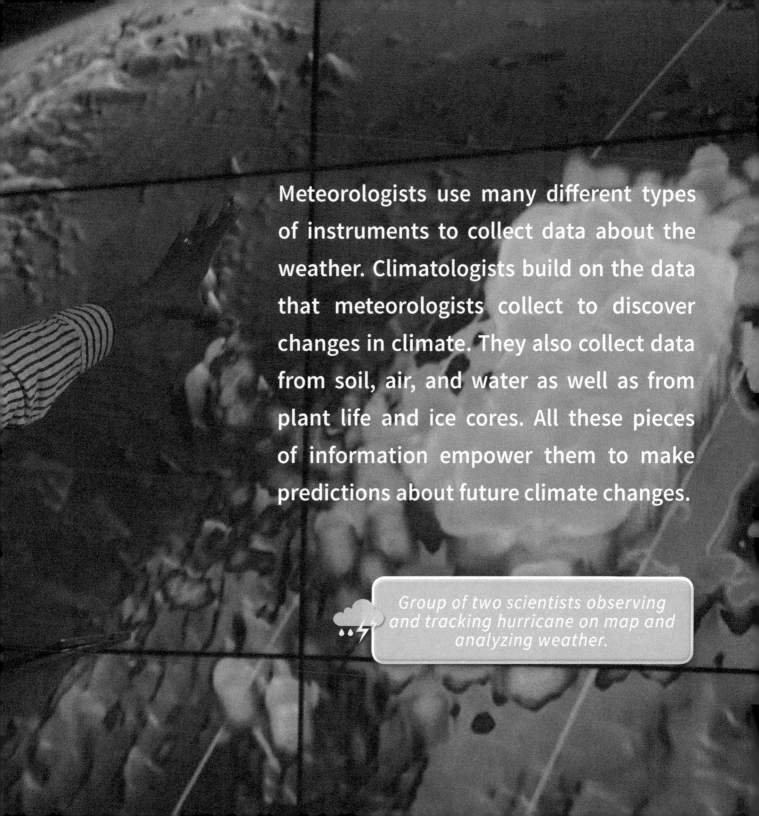

Meteorologists use many different types of instruments to collect data about the weather. Climatologists build on the data that meteorologists collect to discover changes in climate. They also collect data from soil, air, and water as well as from plant life and ice cores. All these pieces of information empower them to make predictions about future climate changes.

Group of two scientists observing and tracking hurricane on map and analyzing weather.

Awesome! Now that you've learned about the differences between climate and weather you may want to read about storms in the Baby Professor **book**, *Chasing Storms and Other Weather Disturbances - Weather for Kids | Children's Earth Sciences Books.*

Visit

www.BabyProfessorBooks.com

to download Free Baby Professor eBooks and view
our catalog of new and exciting Children's Books

CPSIA information can be obtained
at www.ICGtesting.com
Printed in the USA
BVHW012328101220
595458BV00016B/534

9 781541 949423